Pedro Martinez

by A. R. Schaefer

Reading Consultant:
Dr. Robert Miller
Professor of Special Education
Minnesota State University, Mankato

CAPSTONE
HIGH-INTEREST
BOOKS

an imprint of Capstone Press
Mankato, Minnesota

Capstone High-Interest Books are published by Capstone Press
151 Good Counsel Drive, P.O. Box 669, Mankato, Minnesota 56002
http://www.capstone-press.com

Library of Congress Cataloging-in-Publication Data
Schaefer, A. R. (Adam Richard), 1976–
    Pedro Martinez/by A.R. Schaefer.
    p. cm.—(Sports heroes)
    Summary: A brief biography of the Boston Red Sox pitcher who won the
Cy Young Award in 1997 and 1999.
    ISBN 0-7368-1296-2 (hardcover)
    1. Martinez, Pedro, 1971—Juvenile literature. 2. Baseball players—Dominican
Republic—Biography—Juvenile literature. [1. Martinez, Pedro, 1971– 2. Baseball
players.] I. Title. II. Sports heroes (Mankato, Minn.)
GV865.M355 S32 2003
796.357'092—dc21   2001008186

Editorial Credits
Matt Doeden, editor; Karen Risch, product planning editor; Timothy Halldin, series
    designer; Gene Bentdahl, book designer; Jo Miller, photo researcher

Photo Credits
AP Wide World Photos/Jim Rogash, 15; Chris O'Meara, 38
Getty Images/David Seelig, cover; Jonathan Daniel, 4; Matthew Stockman, 7;
    Steve Babineau, 9, 41, 42; Brian Bahr, 10; Steve Dunn, 17, 23; J. D. Cuban, 18;
    Otto Greule Jr., 24; Jose L. Marin, 27; Al Bello, 31; Jeff Gross, 33; Rick Berk, 36
Bettmann/Corbis, 12
SportsChrome-USA, 28; Michael Zito, 21; Rob Tringali Jr., 34

1 2 3 4 5 6 07 06 05 04 03 02

Table of Contents

Features

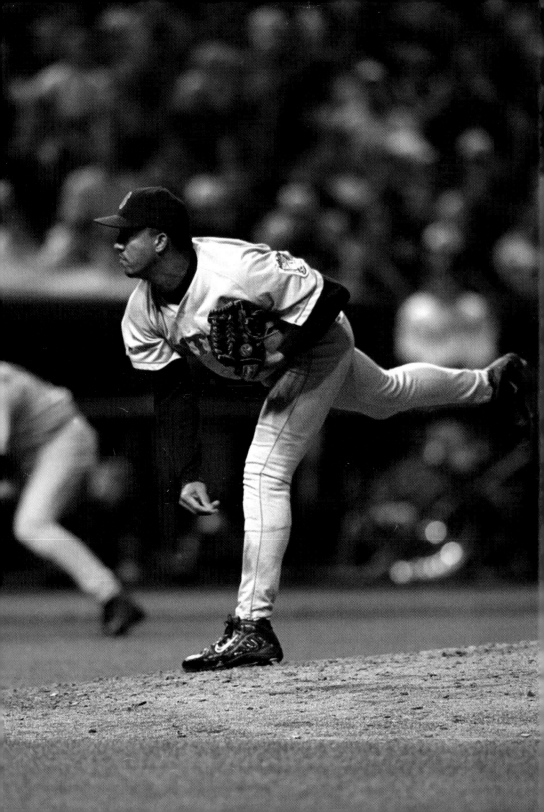

CHAPTER 1

Playoff Ace

On October 11, 1999, the Boston Red Sox and the Cleveland Indians were playing a first-round playoff game at Jacobs Field in Cleveland, Ohio. The series was tied 2-2. The winner of the fifth game would advance to the American League Championship Series (ALCS).

More than 45,000 Indians fans cheered as their team scored eight runs in the game's first three innings. The Red Sox were in trouble. Manager Jimy Williams had already used two pitchers in the game. Neither pitcher could stop the Indians.

Pedro pitched six hitless innings of relief against the Indians in the 1999 playoffs.

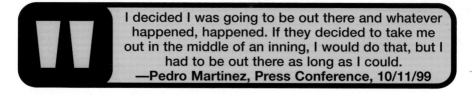

Boston's star pitcher was Pedro Martinez. Pedro had not pitched since the first game of the series. He had hurt his back during that game. Pedro told Williams that he could pitch. Williams knew the season would be over if the Red Sox lost. He decided to let Pedro pitch one or two innings.

Indians fans were surprised to see Pedro walk to the mound. Pedro was a starter. The fans had not expected him to pitch in relief.

Two innings passed. Pedro had not allowed a hit. He told Williams that he wanted to stay in the game. After six innings, the score was tied. During the top of the seventh inning, Troy O'Leary hit a three-run home run for the Red Sox. They were ahead 11-8.

The Red Sox scored another run in the top of the ninth inning. They were ahead 12-8. Pedro then pitched the ninth inning to finish the game. He had pitched six innings in relief without allowing a hit. The Red Sox had won the series.

Pedro celebrated with his teammates after he got the last out of the game.

6

About Pedro Martinez

Pedro Martinez is a starting pitcher for the Boston Red Sox. He has played for the Red Sox since 1998. Before that, he played for the Los Angeles Dodgers and the Montreal Expos.

Pedro is one of the most dominant pitchers in the major leagues. He has won the Cy Young Award three times. He has an excellent fastball that can reach speeds of almost 100 miles (160 kilometers) per hour. His breaking pitches have good movement. His curveballs and sliders are among the best in baseball. He also has an effective changeup. Pedro has good control of all of his pitches. He can throw any of his pitches into the corners of the strike zone.

CAREER STATISTICS

Pedro Martinez

Major League Pitching Statistics

Year	Team	Games	W-L	SO	ERA
1992	LA	2	0-1	8	2.25
1993	LA	65	10-5	119	2.61
1994	MON	24	11-5	142	3.42
1995	MON	30	14-10	174	3.51
1996	MON	33	13-10	222	3.70
1997	MON	31	17-8	305	1.90
1998	BOS	33	19-7	251	2.89
1999	BOS	31	23-4	313	2.07
2000	BOS	29	18-6	284	1.74
2001	BOS	18	7-3	163	2.39
Career		296	132-59	1,981	2.66

CHAPTER 2

The Early Years

Pedro Martinez was born October 25, 1971, in Manoguayabo, Dominican Republic. This country is located on the island of Hispaniola in the Caribbean Sea. Manoguayabo is a small town near the capital city of Santo Domingo. Pedro's parents are Paulino and Leopoldina Martinez. He has three brothers and two sisters.

Pedro's Childhood

Pedro took school seriously. He knew that he needed an education to get a good job. He got good grades. English was one of his favorite

Pedro was born October 25, 1971.

A Hero's Hero

Juan Marichal

As a child, Pedro's baseball heroes included his father and his brother Ramon. His favorite player outside of his family was Juan Marichal. Marichal pitched in the major leagues from 1960 to 1975. Like Pedro, he was from the Dominican Republic.

Marichal played for the San Francisco Giants for 14 years. He also played for the Dodgers. He won 243 games during his career. He won more than 25 games in a season three times during the 1960s.

Marichal retired from baseball in 1975. Eight years later, he was elected into baseball's Hall of Fame.

Marichal was present when Pedro received the Cy Young Award in 1997. Marichal never won the Cy Young Award. Many baseball experts believe he should have. Pedro wanted to give his award to Marichal. But Marichal would not accept it. He wanted Pedro to keep it.

subjects. Spanish is the main language of the Dominican Republic. But Pedro also wanted to speak English well.

Baseball was important to the Martinez family. The San Francisco Giants had once asked Paulino to try out for their team. But he did not have enough money to buy equipment for the tryout.

Pedro's three brothers were all good pitchers. Ramon, Nelson, and Jesus all were tall and strong boys. Pedro was smaller. He thought his small size would prevent him from pitching as well as his brothers.

Pedro still played baseball whenever he got a chance. But he did not have enough money to buy baseball equipment. He often played with rocks, rolled-up socks, or fruit. He sometimes even broke the heads off of his sisters' dolls to use as baseballs.

Discovered by the Dodgers
In 1984, Ramon was chosen to pitch for the Dominican Olympic baseball team. Ramon

traveled to Los Angeles, California, with the team. After the Olympics, the Los Angeles Dodgers signed Ramon to a contract.

The Dodgers sent Ramon to train with a team in Santo Domingo. Pedro went along. One day, one of the Dodgers' pitching coaches timed Pedro's fastball. It was very fast for Pedro's age. The coach told Pedro that he could be a professional pitcher if he worked hard.

Pedro practiced and learned about pitching from Ramon. In 1988, Pedro signed a minor league contract with the Dodgers. For the next two seasons, he worked with the Dodgers' coaches in the Dominican Republic.

Pedro attended Ohio Dominican College while he trained. He was a good student. Pedro took more English classes. He wanted to speak English well when he moved to the United States.

Minor League Baseball

In 1990, the Dodgers asked Pedro to join their minor league team in Great Falls,

Pedro learned a great deal about pitching in the major leagues from his brother Ramon.

Montana. Pedro pitched well that year. He had an 8-3 record. He struck out 82 batters in only 77 innings. He was named to the league's All-Star team.

In 1991, the Dodgers sent Pedro to their Class A team in Bakersfield, California. Pedro had an 8-0 record in 10 starts. His ERA was 2.05. The Dodgers were very pleased with his performance. They moved him to their Class AA team in San Antonio, Texas.

Pedro continued to pitch well in San Antonio. He had an ERA of 1.76. But the team did not score many runs. Pedro's record was only 7-5. The Dodgers knew that Pedro had pitched well. Near the end of the season, they promoted Pedro to their Class AAA team in Albuquerque, New Mexico. The team is called the Dukes.

Pedro went 3-3 in six games for the Dukes. For the entire season, Pedro's record was 18-8. He struck out 192 batters. *The Sporting News* named him Minor League Player of the Year.

Pedro hoped to play in the major leagues in 1992. Ramon was already playing for the Dodgers. But the Dodgers wanted Pedro to spend another season with the Dukes. He had a 7-6 record that season. In September, the Dodgers called Pedro up to the majors.

Pedro began his major league career with the Dodgers in September 1992.

The Major Leagues

Pedro's first major league game was September 24 against the Cincinnati Reds. Pedro came into the game as a relief pitcher. He pitched two scoreless innings. Six days later, Pedro got his first major league start against the Reds. He gave up only two runs in six innings. But the Dodgers lost the game 3-1.

Rookie Year

Pedro reported to the Dodgers' spring training before the 1993 season. He pitched very well. He thought he would make the major league

Pedro pitched in 65 games for the Dodgers in 1993.

team. But before the season, the Dodgers sent him back to Albuquerque. Pedro was very disappointed. He thought about retiring. But Ramon talked him out of quitting.

Pedro pitched only one game for the Dukes in 1993. The Dodgers then decided that they wanted Pedro on the major league team. They asked him to be a relief pitcher. Pedro was used to being a starter. But he was still happy to be joining Ramon in Los Angeles.

Pedro pitched in 65 games for the Dodgers in 1993. He finished with a 10-5 record and an ERA of 2.61. He also struck out 119 batters in 107 innings. On April 11, Pedro came into a game to relieve Ramon. It was the first time in almost 14 years that brothers had pitched in the same major league game.

Traded to Montreal

After the 1993 season, the Dodgers traded Pedro to the Montreal Expos for second baseman Delino Deshields. The Expos were one of baseball's worst teams. At first, Pedro

The Dodgers traded Pedro to the Montreal Expos after the 1993 season.

was disappointed. He was sad to leave his brother. But he was excited about the opportunity to be a starter for the Expos.

Pedro started the 1994 season well. On April 13, he gave up only one hit in eight innings. The Expos also played well as a team. They led their division late in the season. But the baseball players went on strike in August. They were unhappy with the way baseball owners treated them. The rest of the 1994 season was canceled. Pedro ended the year with an 11-5 record.

Many baseball experts thought the Expos would have another good season in 1995. But the team did not do well. Pedro still had a good year. He went 14-10 with an ERA of 3.51.

On June 3, Pedro took a perfect game into the ninth inning against the San Diego Padres. Padre outfielder Bip Roberts hit a double to lead off the ninth inning. The hit ruined Pedro's try for a perfect game. But the Expos still won the game 1-0.

Pedro finished the 1995 season with a 14-10 record.

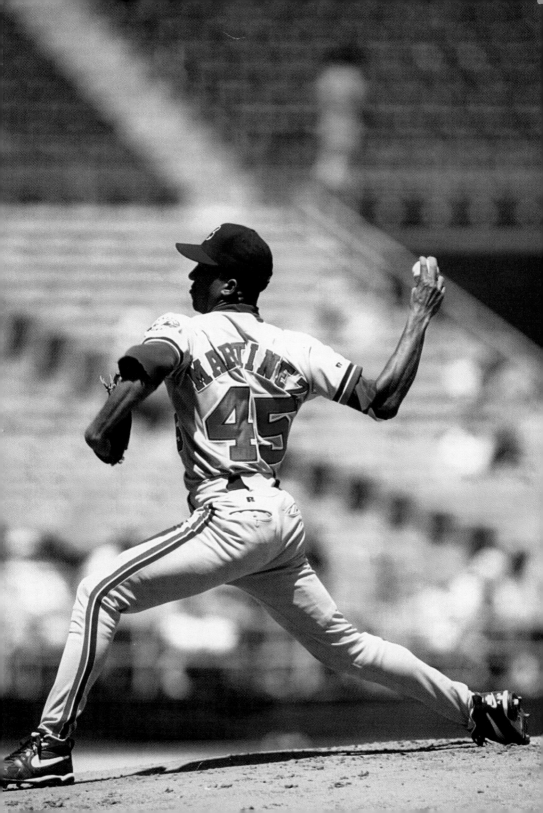

CHAPTER 4

Cy Young Awards

Pedro finished the 1996 season with a 13-10 record. His 3.70 ERA was the worst of his career. The Expos finished the season with a record of 88-74. The team did not make the playoffs.

Pedro was disappointed with his season. He knew he could do better. He wanted to prove that he was one of the best pitchers in the major leagues.

Pedro's 3.70 ERA in 1996 was the worst of his career.

Cy Young Award Winner

Pedro had a great season in 1997. He led the National League with an ERA of 1.90. He also had 305 strikeouts. He became only the fifth N.L. pitcher since 1900 to strike out more than 300 batters.

The Expos played poorly in 1997. They did not score many runs in the games Pedro started. Pedro's record for the season was only 17-8.

Pedro received many awards for his excellent season. He was named to the National League All-Star team in July. After the season, he was named the N.L. Cy Young Award winner and *The Sporting News* N.L. Pitcher of the Year.

Another Trade

The Expos were having trouble bringing fans in to see their games. The owners did not make much money from the team. Many of the team's young stars left Montreal as free agents.

In 1997, Pedro became only the fifth N.L. pitcher since 1900 to strike out more than 300 batters.

Pedro had only one year left on his contract. Expos officials knew they could not afford to sign him to a new contract. On November 18, 1997, the Expos traded Pedro to the Boston Red Sox for pitchers Carl Pavano and Tony Armas Jr.

Pedro was excited to join the Red Sox. They were a much better team than the Expos. Pedro knew that the Red Sox would give him better run support than the Expos had. He also knew that he had a better chance to reach the playoffs with the Red Sox.

In December, Pedro and the Red Sox agreed to a new six-year contract worth $75 million. At the time, the contract made Pedro the highest-paid player in baseball.

Red Sox fans were happy to have Pedro on the team. Hundreds of fans waited at the airport to greet Pedro on his first trip to Boston. Pedro did not disappoint his new fans. In 1998, he went 19-7 and had 251 strikeouts. He helped the Red Sox advance to the playoffs. He also won his only playoff start.

Pedro joined the Red Sox in 1998.

The Red Sox did not advance past the first round of the playoffs. But Pedro was still pleased with his season.

Baseball's Best Pitcher

In 1999, Pedro proved that he was the best pitcher in baseball. He finished the season with a 23-4 record and an ERA of 2.07. He also struck out 313 batters. He was named American League Pitcher of the Month in April, May, June, and September. An injury prevented him from playing during parts of July and August.

On July 13, Pedro was the starting pitcher for the American League in the All-Star Game. He struck out five of the six batters he faced. His performance earned him the All-Star Game MVP trophy.

Pedro pitched even better during the playoffs. He pitched both as a starter and as a reliever during Boston's first-round series with the Indians. He also started one game in the ALCS against the New York Yankees.

On July 13, 1999, Pedro was named the MVP of the All-Star Game.

Pedro pitched a total of 17 innings in the playoffs. He gave up only three hits and did not allow any runs. But his performance was not enough to help the Red Sox advance to the World Series.

After the season, Pedro was named the A.L. Cy Young Award winner. He also finished second in the A.L. Most Valuable Player (MVP) Award voting. Pitchers rarely finish that high in the voting. The Associated Press named Pedro the Major League Player of the Year.

Pedro continued his success in 2000. The Red Sox did not play as well as they had in 1999. But Pedro remained the best pitcher in baseball. He had an 18-6 record and an ERA of 1.74. His ERA was the lowest in Red Sox history. Pedro again won the Cy Young Award. He became the seventh pitcher to win the award three times.

Pedro won his third Cy Young Award in 2000.

CHAPTER 5

Pedro Martinez Today

The 2001 season started well for Pedro. At the end of May, he was 7-1 with a 1.44 ERA. He had struck out 121 batters in only 81 innings. He appeared to be on his way to a fourth Cy Young Award.

In June, Pedro started to feel pain in his shoulder. It was sore and swelled up after he pitched. He could not pitch as well as he normally did. The Red Sox did not want to risk injuring their star pitcher. They placed him on the disabled list.

Pedro started the 2001 season with a 7-1 record before injuring his shoulder.

Pedro tried to play again late in the season. He pitched in three games. But he had not fully recovered. His pitches did not have the speed and control that they usually have. In September, the Red Sox let Pedro go to the Dominican Republic to rest and to heal. His season was over.

Pedro had a disagreement with Red Sox general manager Dan Duquette during the season. Duquette said late in the season that Pedro was healthy and that he should be pitching. Pedro said his arm still did not feel healed. He was upset with Duquette for saying he should be pitching. Pedro said that the disagreement made him think about leaving the Red Sox. He also said that it made him think about retiring from baseball.

Pedro's contract with the Red Sox ends after the 2003 season. The Red Sox have an option for the 2004 season. They can decide whether to keep Pedro for that season.

Pedro's contract with the Red Sox ends after the 2003 season.

Off the Field

Pedro and Ramon remain very close. Ramon joined Pedro on the Red Sox during the 1999 and 2000 seasons. But Ramon struggled during the 2000 season. He had a 10-8 record. But his ERA was 6.13. In 2001, Ramon pitched briefly for the Pittsburgh Pirates. But he did not pitch well. He had an 0-2 record. Ramon later decided to retire from baseball.

Pedro also enjoys spending time with his other family members. Many of Pedro's family members live near him in Boston. His brother Jesus pitches in the minor leagues. Pedro also makes many trips to his home in the Dominican Republic.

Pedro donates much of his money to charities. He gives a great deal of this money to organizations in the Dominican Republic. He paid for a new church and a baseball field there. He also paid for a day care center and an orphanage to provide a home for children

Pedro often takes time to sign autographs for fans.

whose parents have died. He also gave 300 computers to schools in Manoguayabo.

Pedro gave more than $100,000 to help the victims of Hurricane Georges. This strong storm hit the Dominican Republic in 1998. It destroyed many homes, churches, and places of business. Pedro wanted to help people rebuild their communities.

Pedro remembers his life before baseball. He and his family had to work very hard to survive. Pedro knows that his baseball talent gives him opportunities many people do not have. He hopes his charity work will help other people improve their lives.

Many baseball experts believe that Pedro will be elected to baseball's Hall of Fame someday.

Career Highlights

1971—Pedro is born on October 25 in Manoguayabo, Dominican Republic.

1984—Pedro's brother Ramon is signed by the Los Angeles Dodgers.

1988—Pedro signs a minor league contract with the Dodgers.

1990—Pedro joins the Dodgers minor league team in Great Falls, Montana.

1991—Pedro plays for three minor league teams; he is named Minor League Player of the Year by *The Sporting News*.

1992—In September, Pedro makes his first major league appearance.

1993—Pedro is traded to the Montreal Expos.

1997—Pedro wins 17 games and the N.L. Cy Young Award; in November, he is traded to the Boston Red Sox.

1999—Pedro wins 23 games and his second Cy Young Award.

2000—Pedro throws four shutouts and has a 1.74 ERA; he wins his third Cy Young Award.

2001—Pedro begins the season 7-1; a shoulder injury prevents him from finishing the season.

Words to Know

contract (KON-trakt)—a legal agreement between a team and a player; contracts determine players' salaries.

hurricane (HUR-uh-kane)—a strong tropical storm that includes heavy rains and very strong winds

option (OP-shuhn)—a part of a contract that allows one side to make a decision without asking the other side; the Red Sox can use their option in Pedro's contract to keep him under contract for the 2004 season.

orphanage (OR-fuh-nij)—a place that provides a home for children whose parents have died

retire (ri-TIRE)—to give up a line of work

strike (STRIKE)—to refuse to work until a set of demands are met

To Learn More

Gallagher, Jim. *Pedro Martinez.* Latinos in Baseball. Childs, Md.: Mitchell Lane Publishers, 1999.

Krasner, Stephen. *Pedro Martinez.* Latinos in the Limelight. Philadelphia: Chelsea House, 2002.

Stewart, Mark. *Pedro Martinez, Pitcher Perfect.* Sports Stars. New York: Children's Press, 2000.

Useful Addresses

Major League Baseball
Office of the Commissioner of Baseball
245 Park Avenue
31st Floor
New York, NY 10167

National Baseball Hall of Fame and Museum
P.O. Box 590
Cooperstown, NY 13326

Pedro Martinez
The Boston Red Sox
Fenway Park
4 Yawkey Way
Boston, MA 02215-3496

Internet Sites

Boston Red Sox
http://redsox.mlb.com

CNNsi.com—Pedro Martinez
http://sportsillustrated.cnn.com/baseball/mlb/
    ml/players/4875/index.html

ESPN.com—Pedro Martinez
http://sports.espn.go.com/mlb/players/
    profile?statsId=4875

Major League Baseball
http://www.mlb.com

Index